Weather

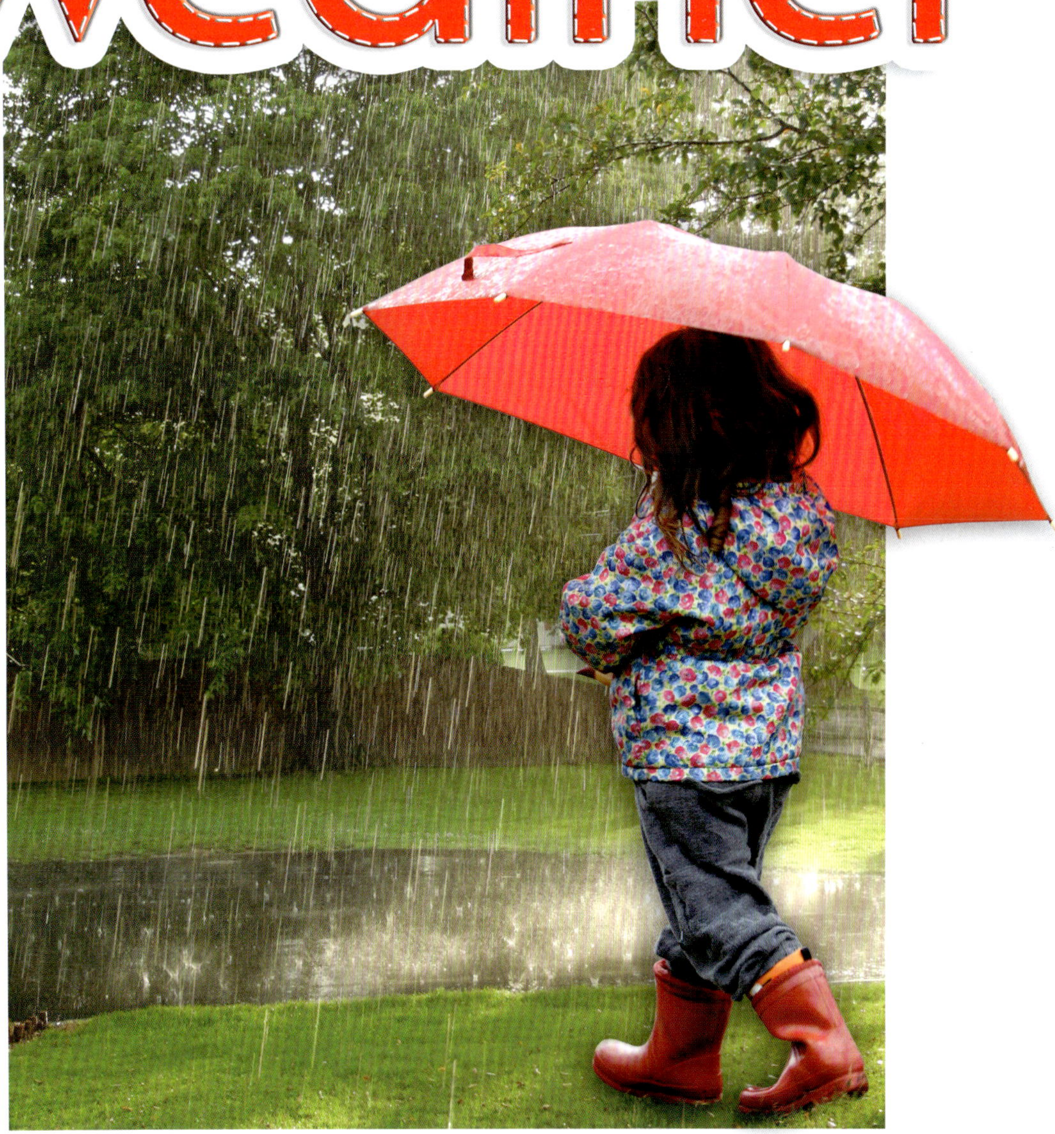

Lee Aucoin

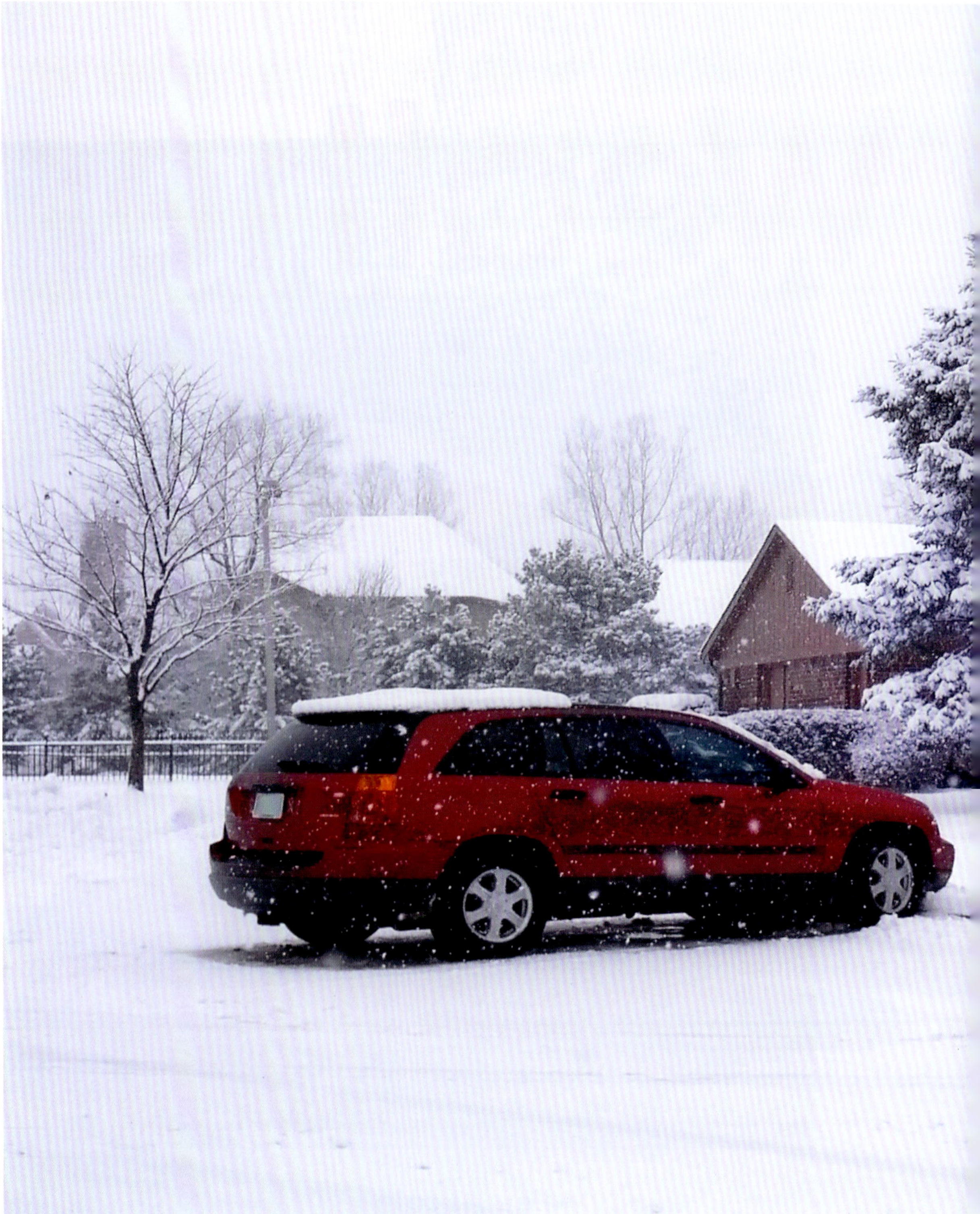

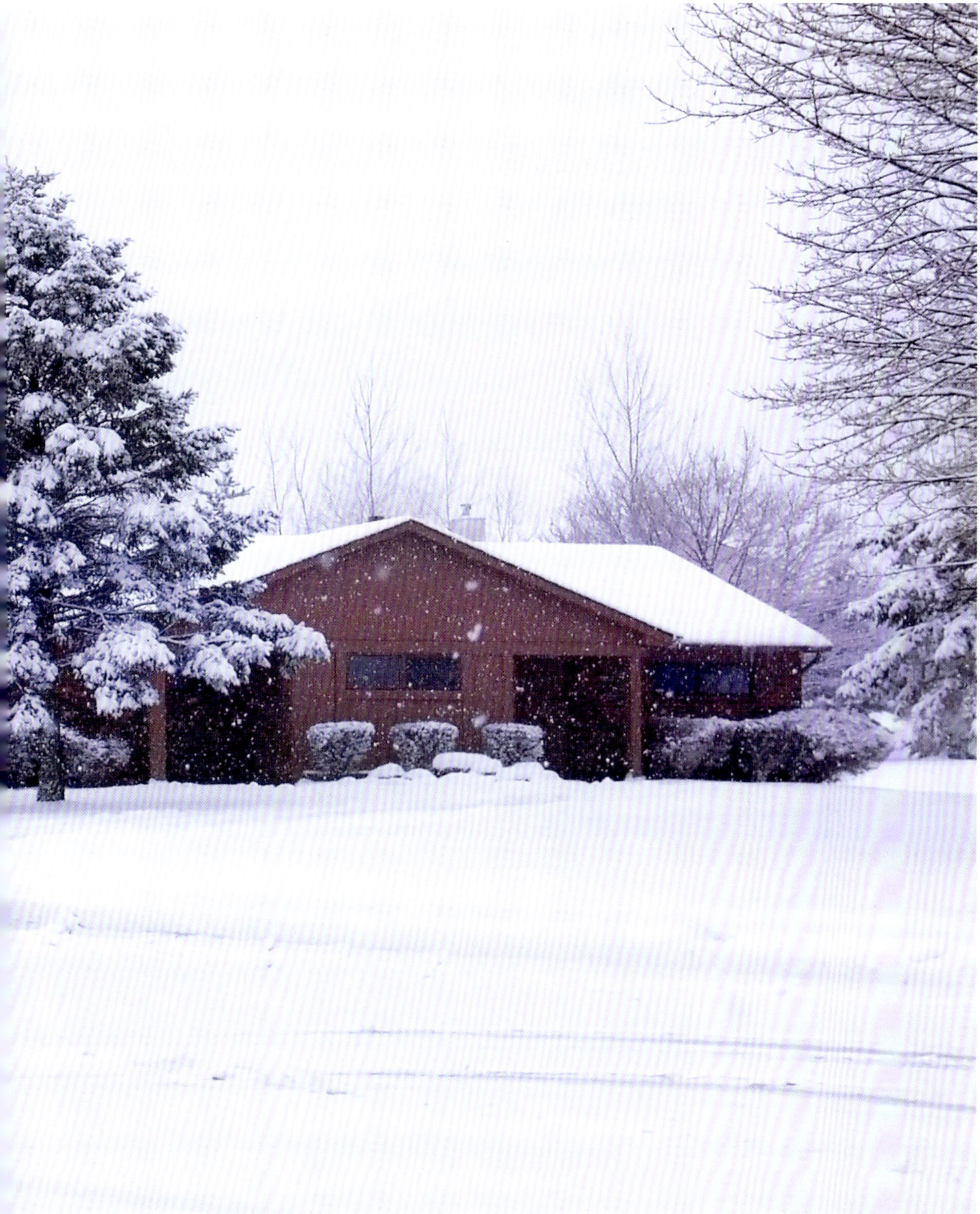

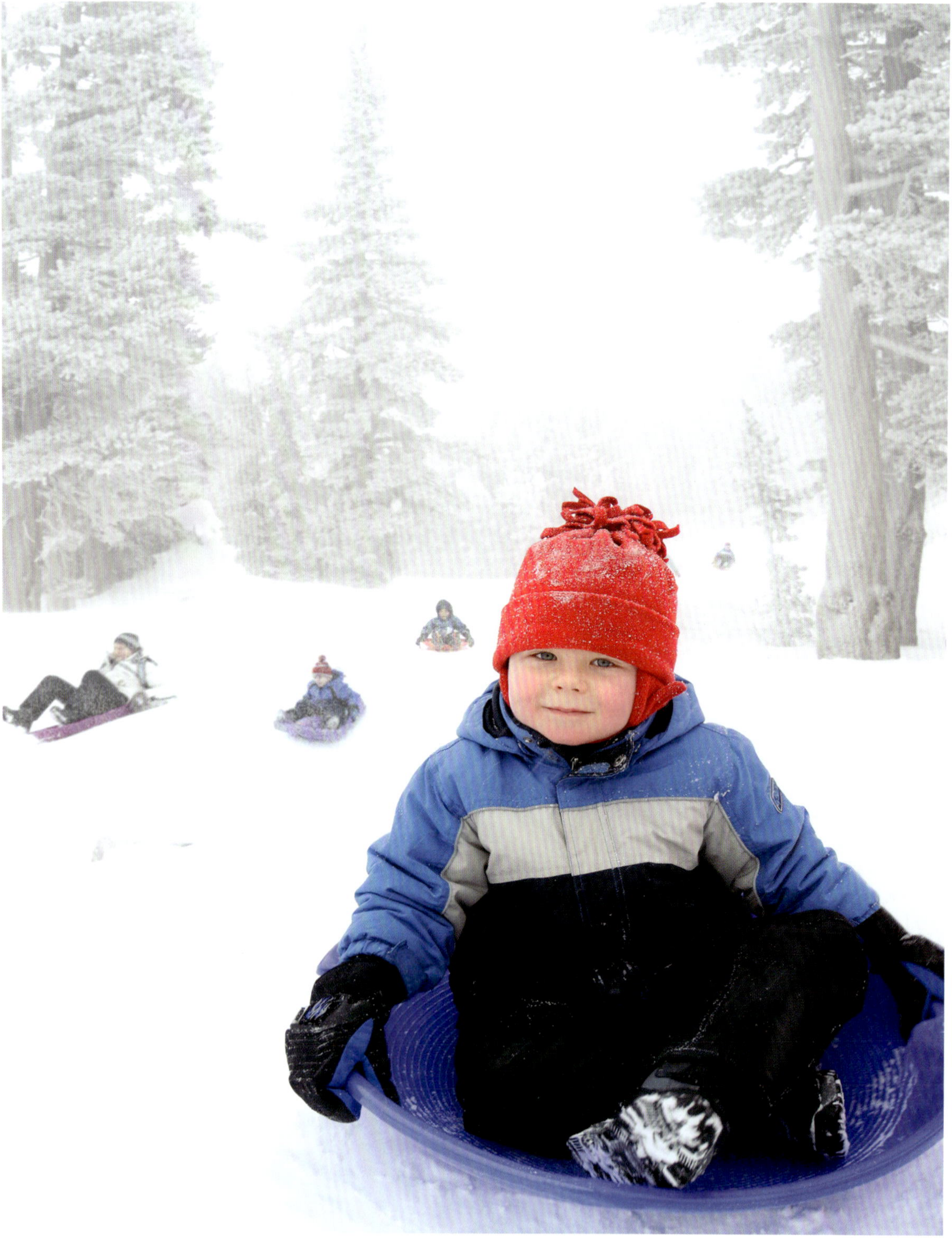

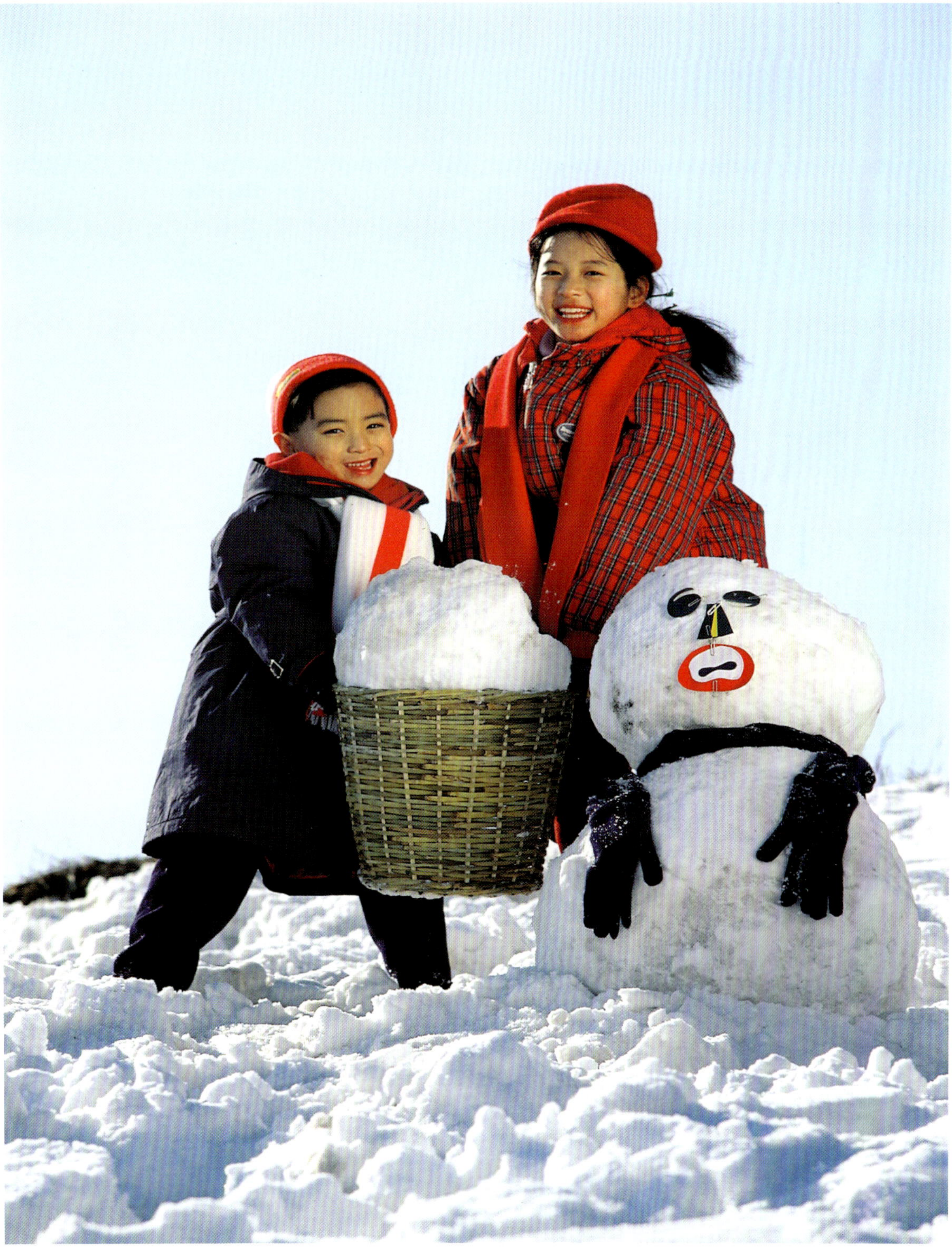

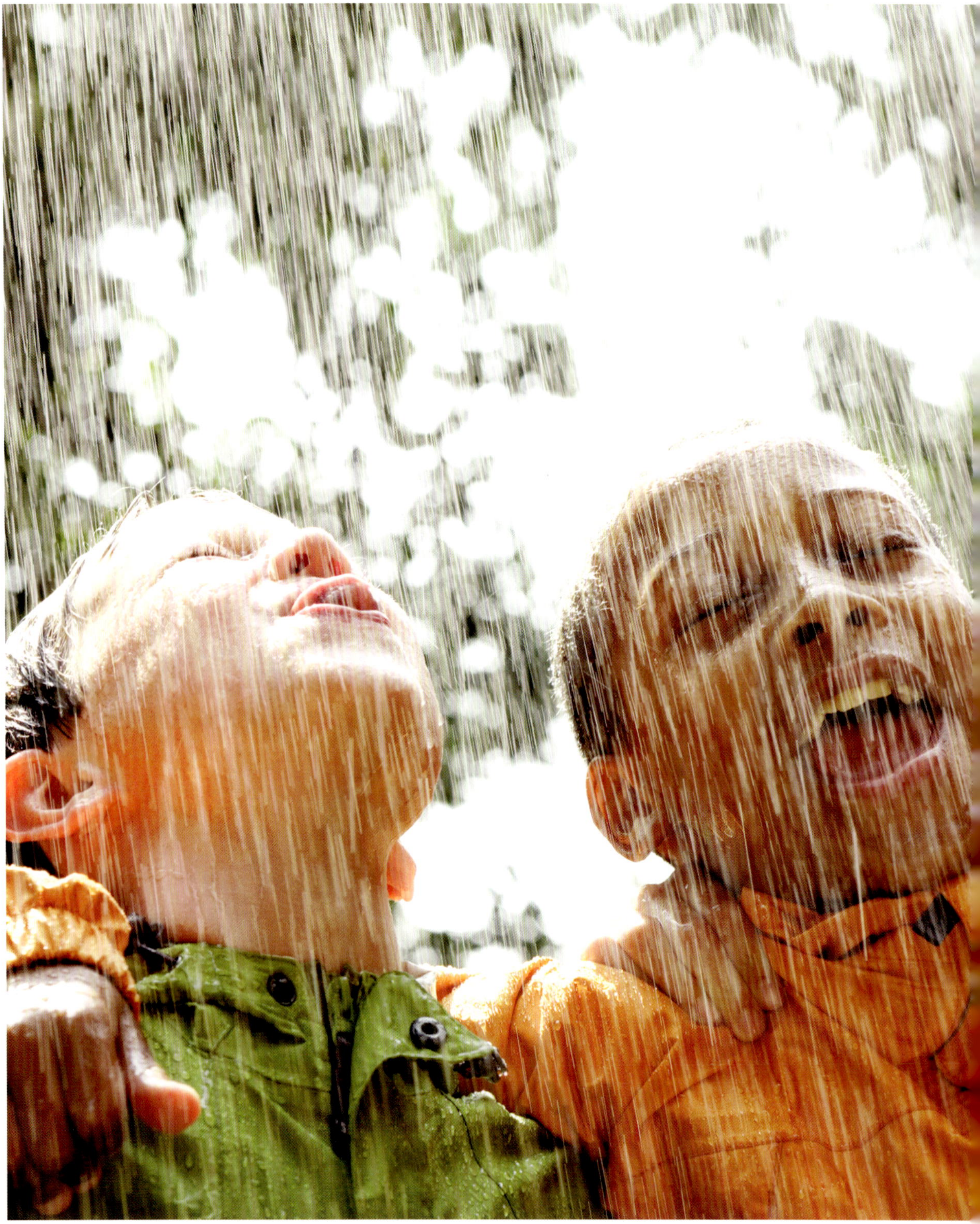

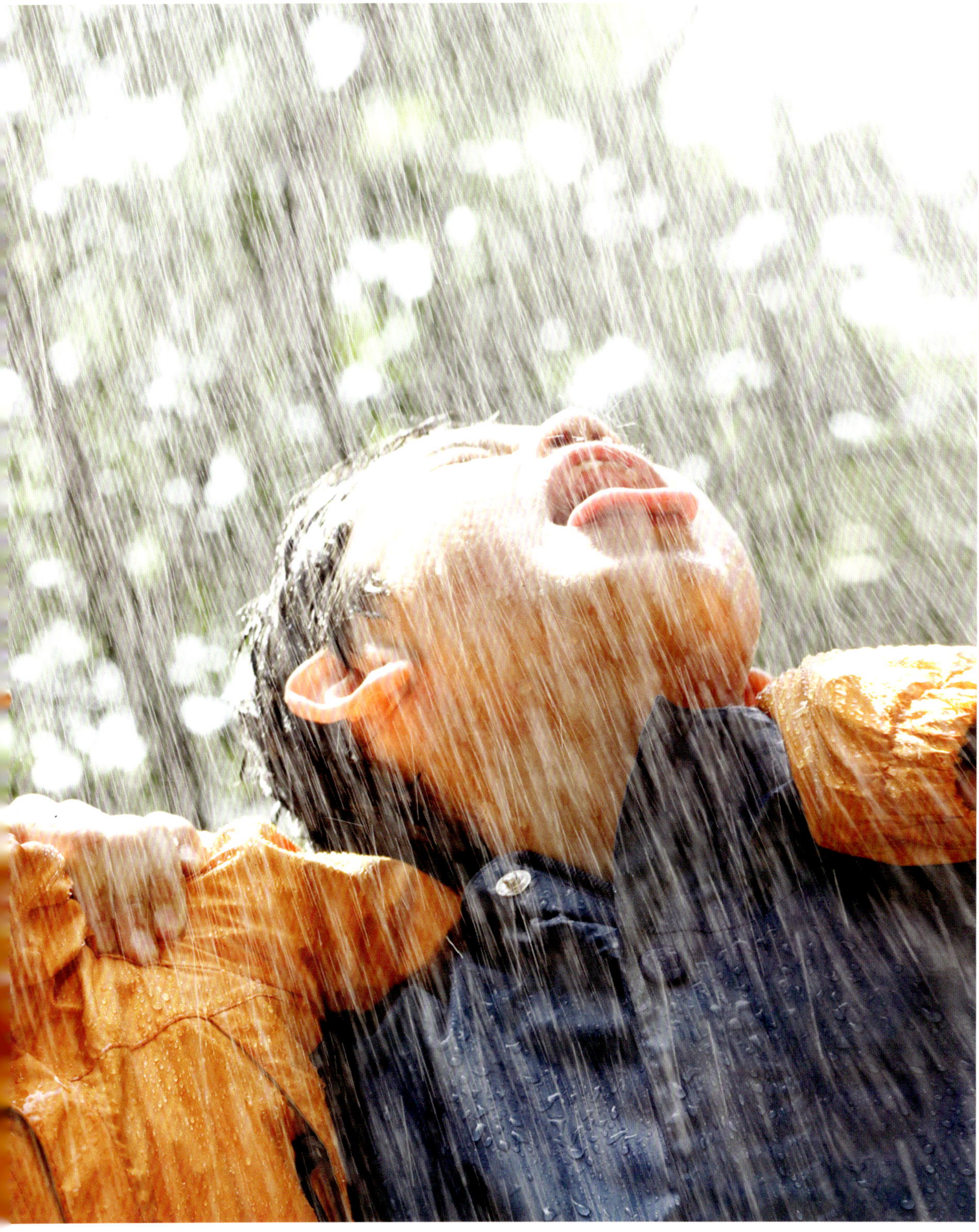

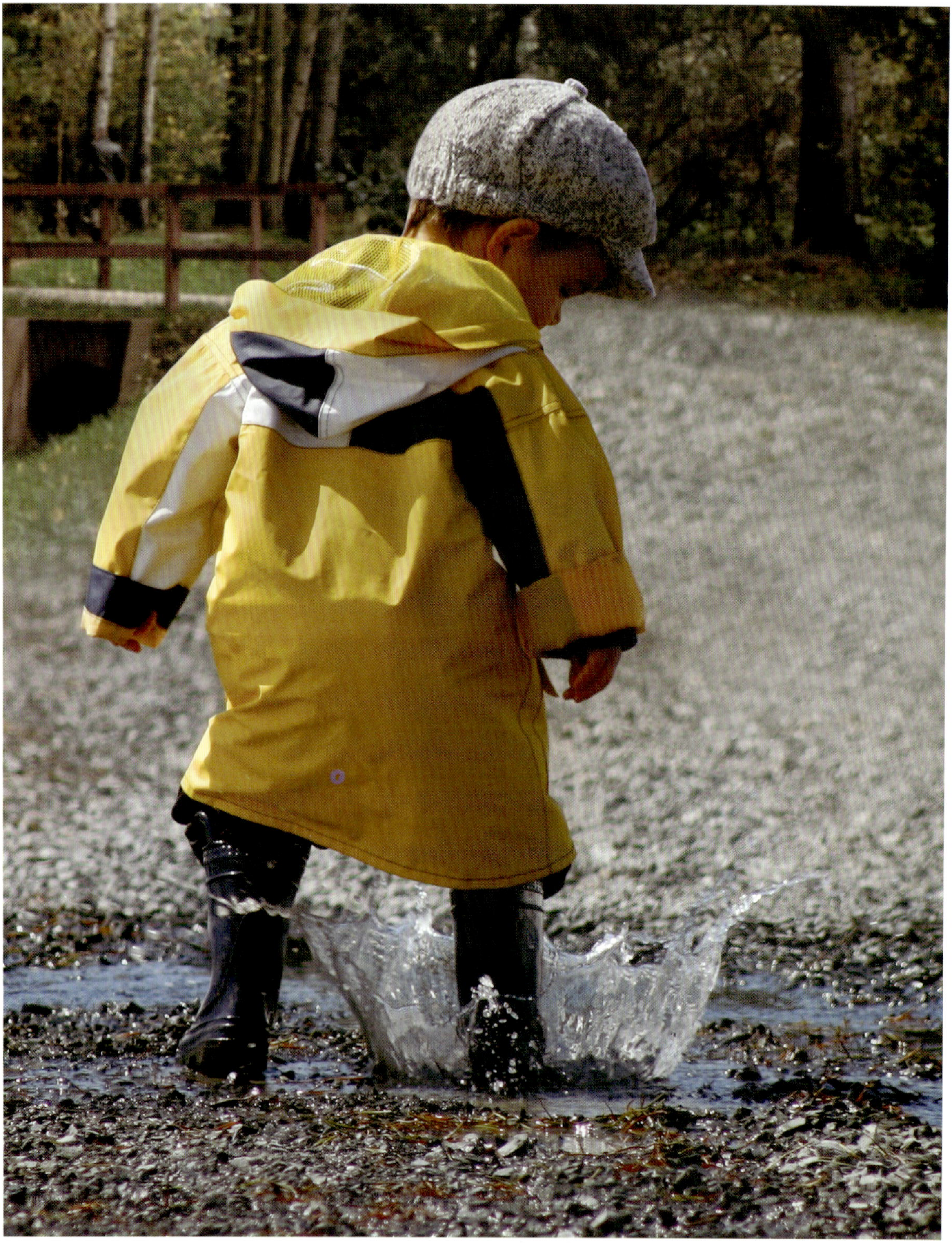

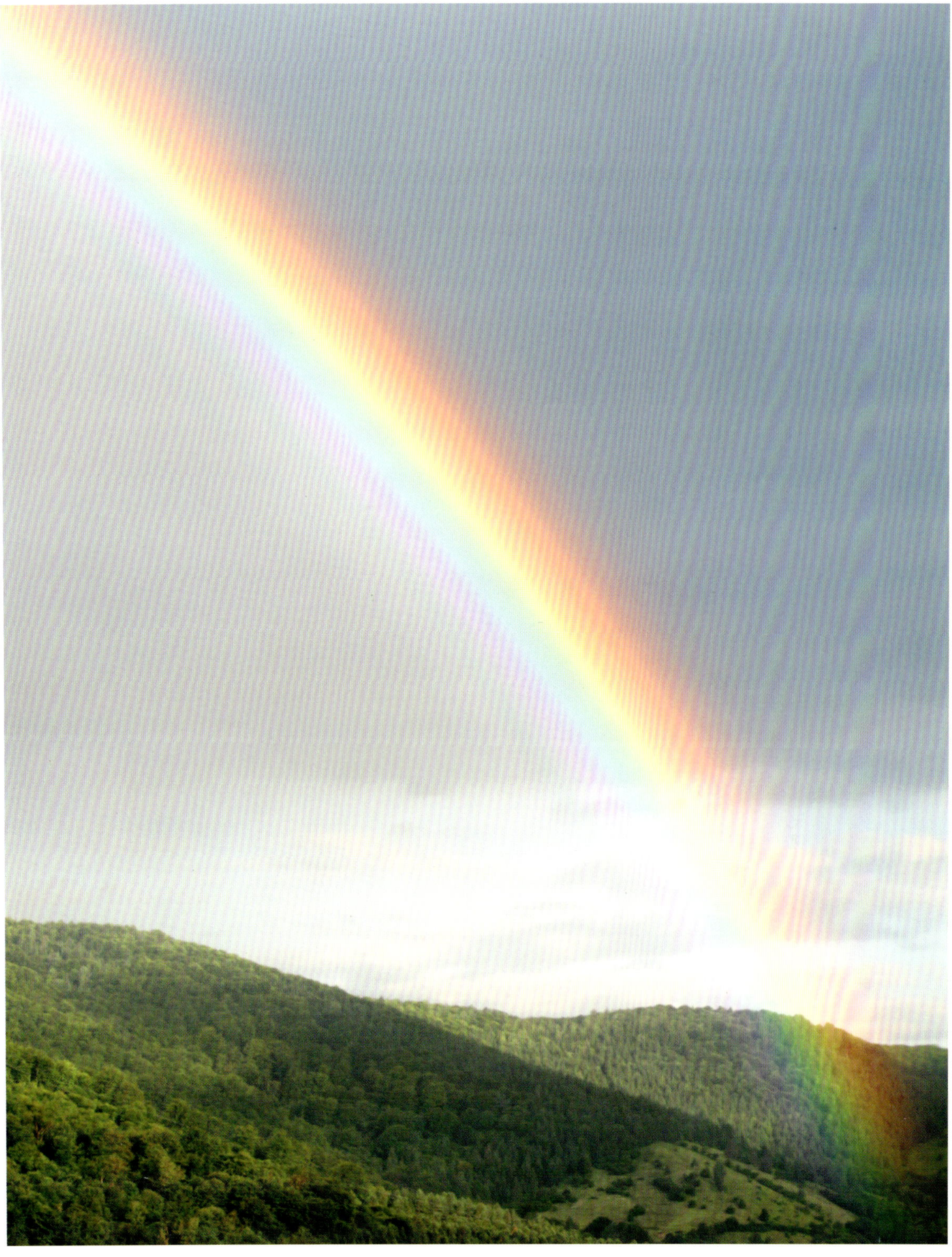

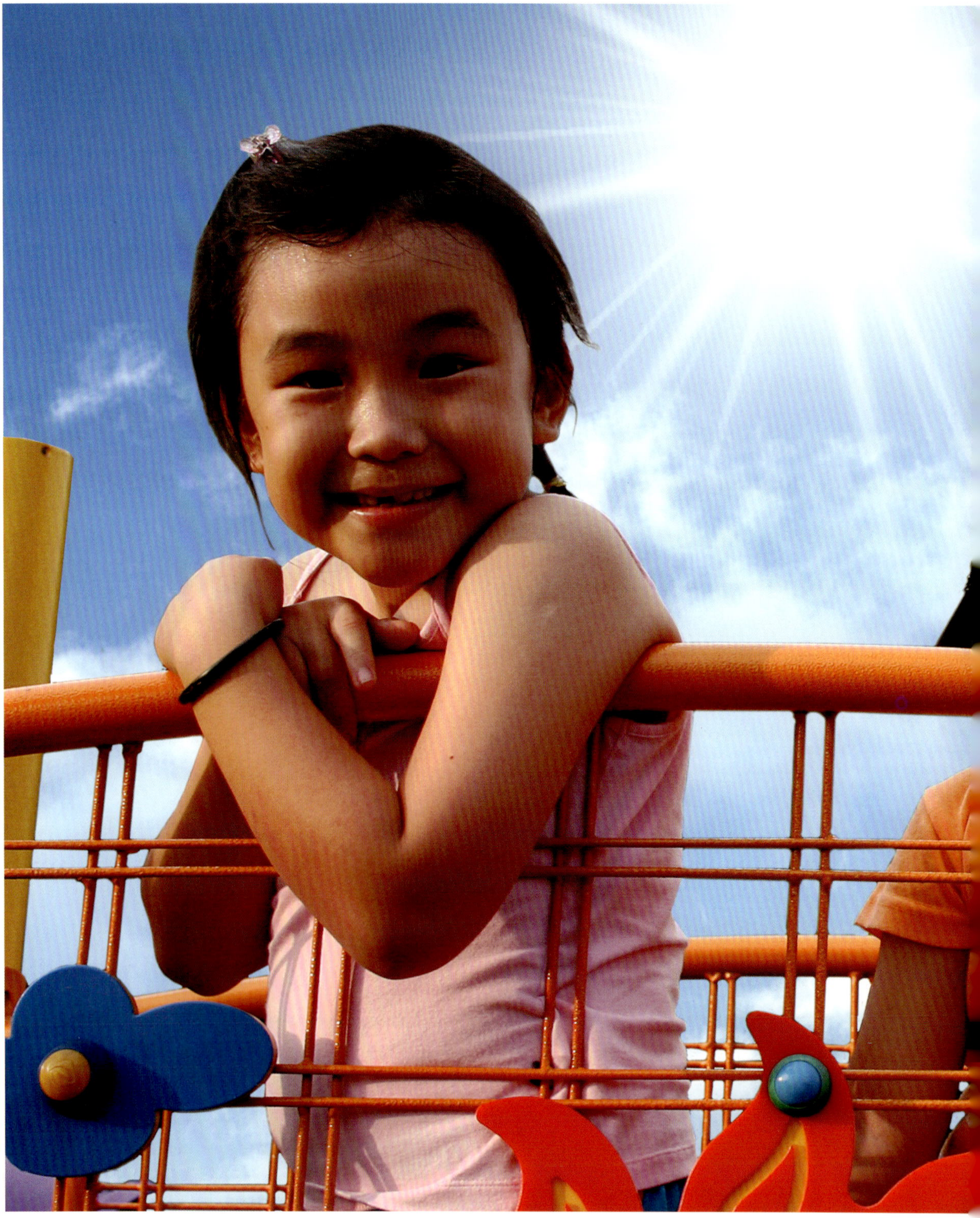

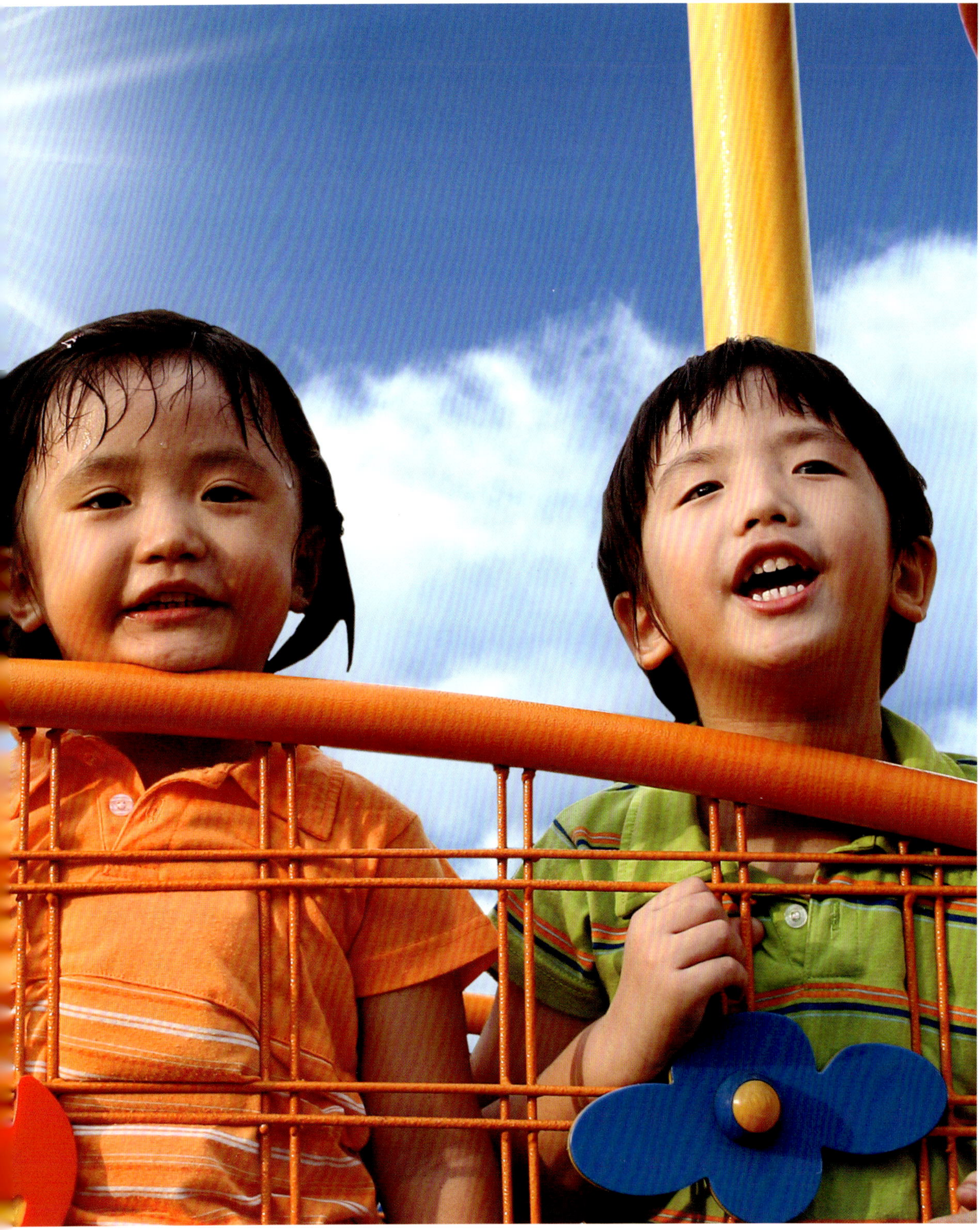

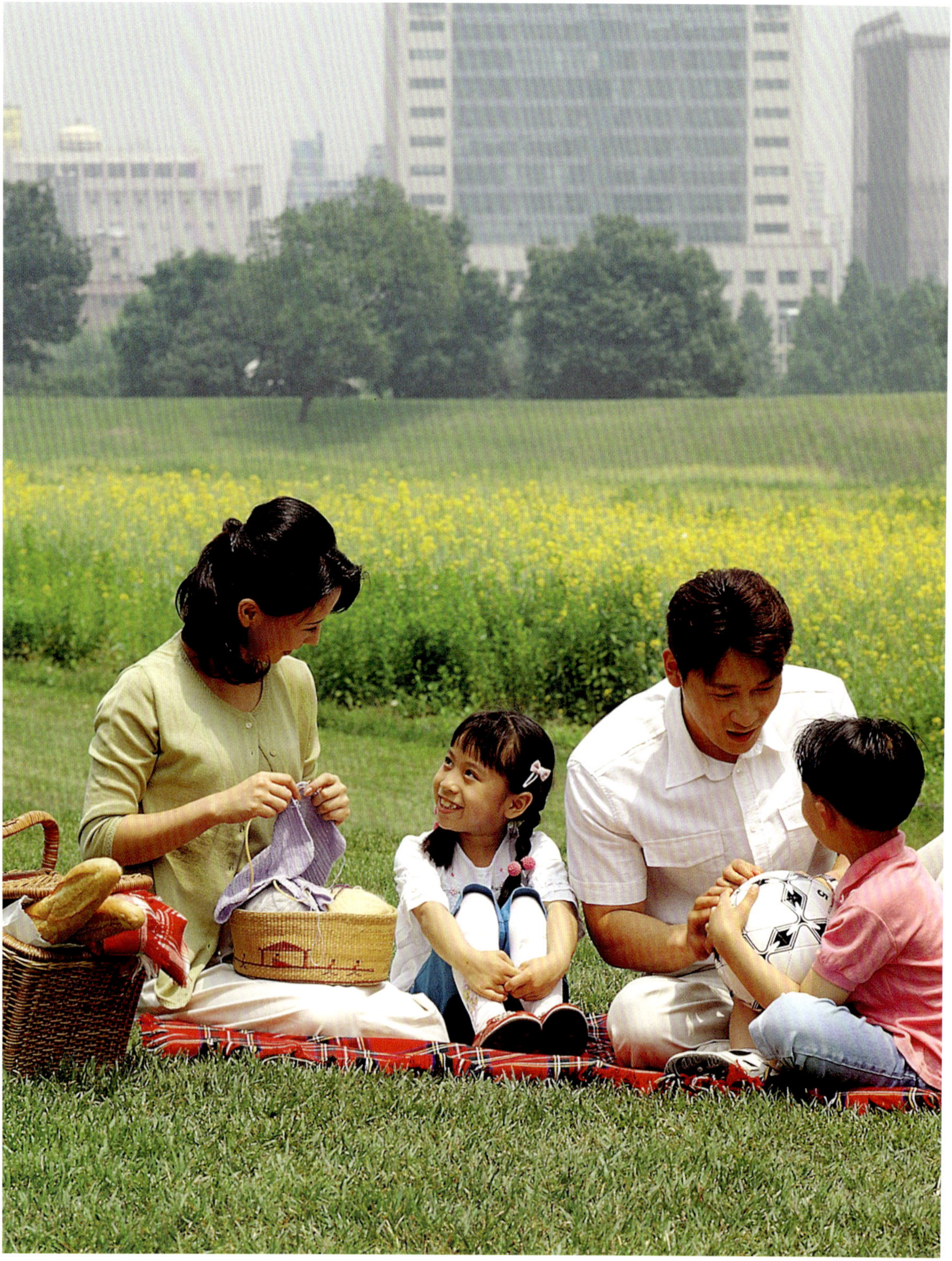

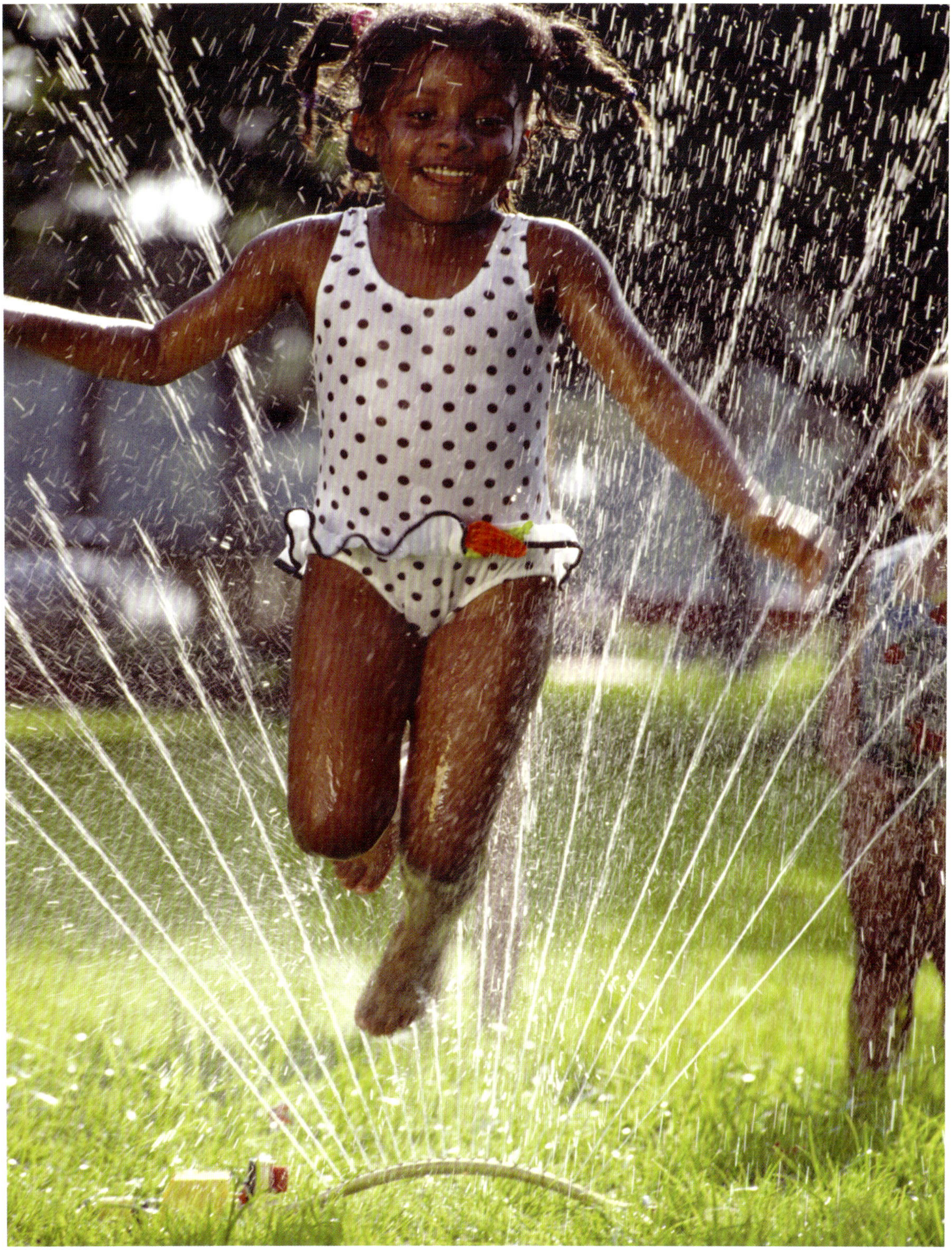

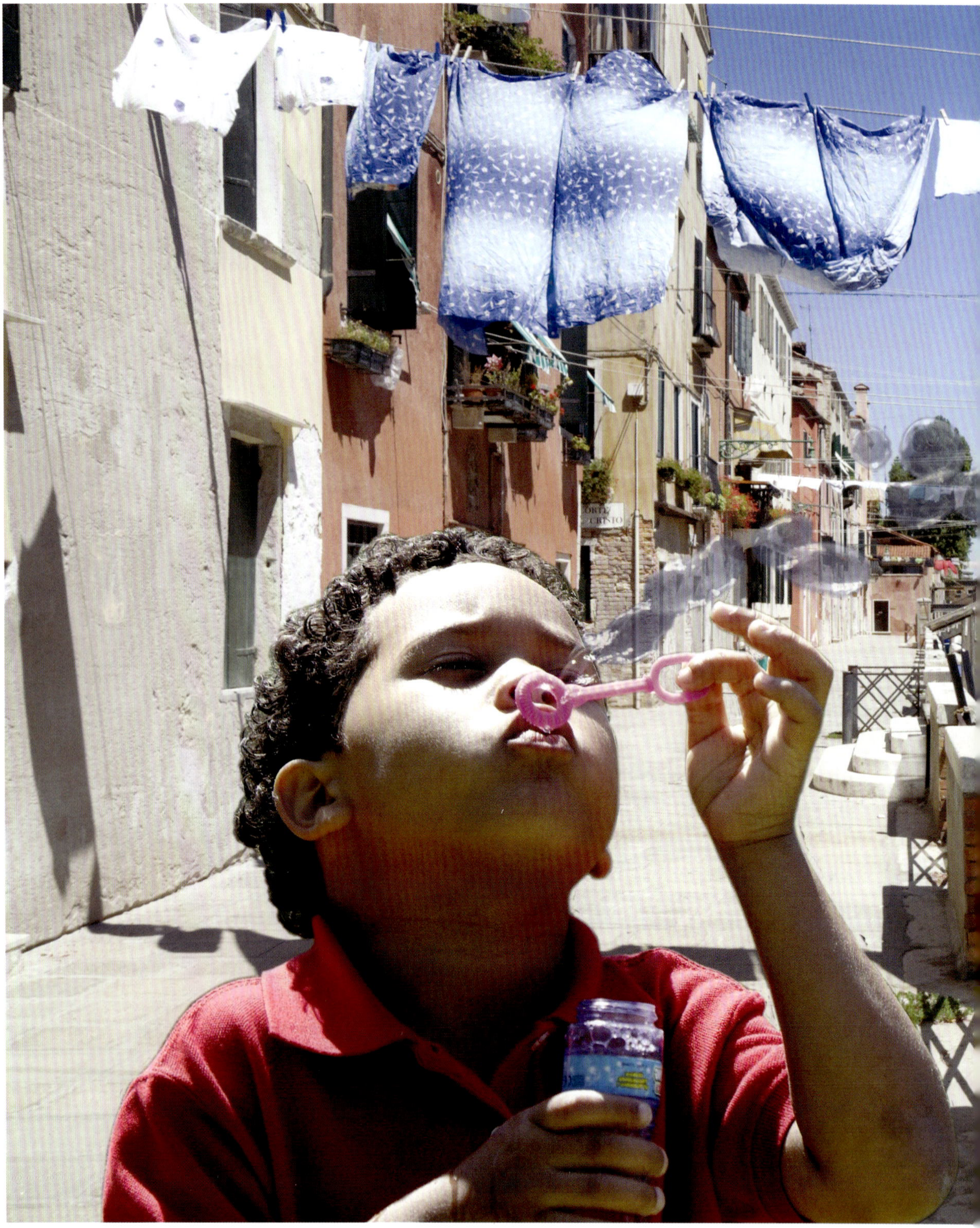

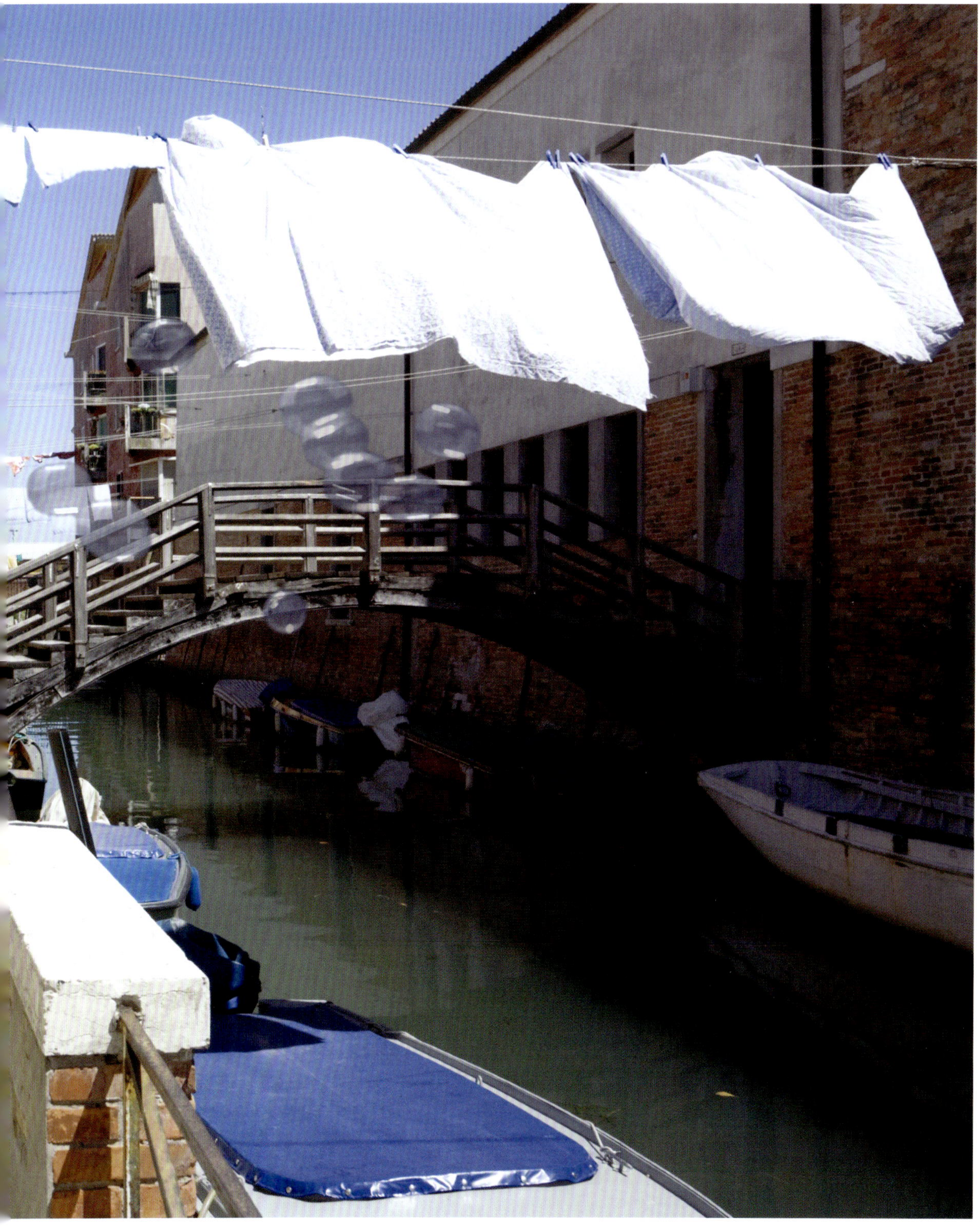

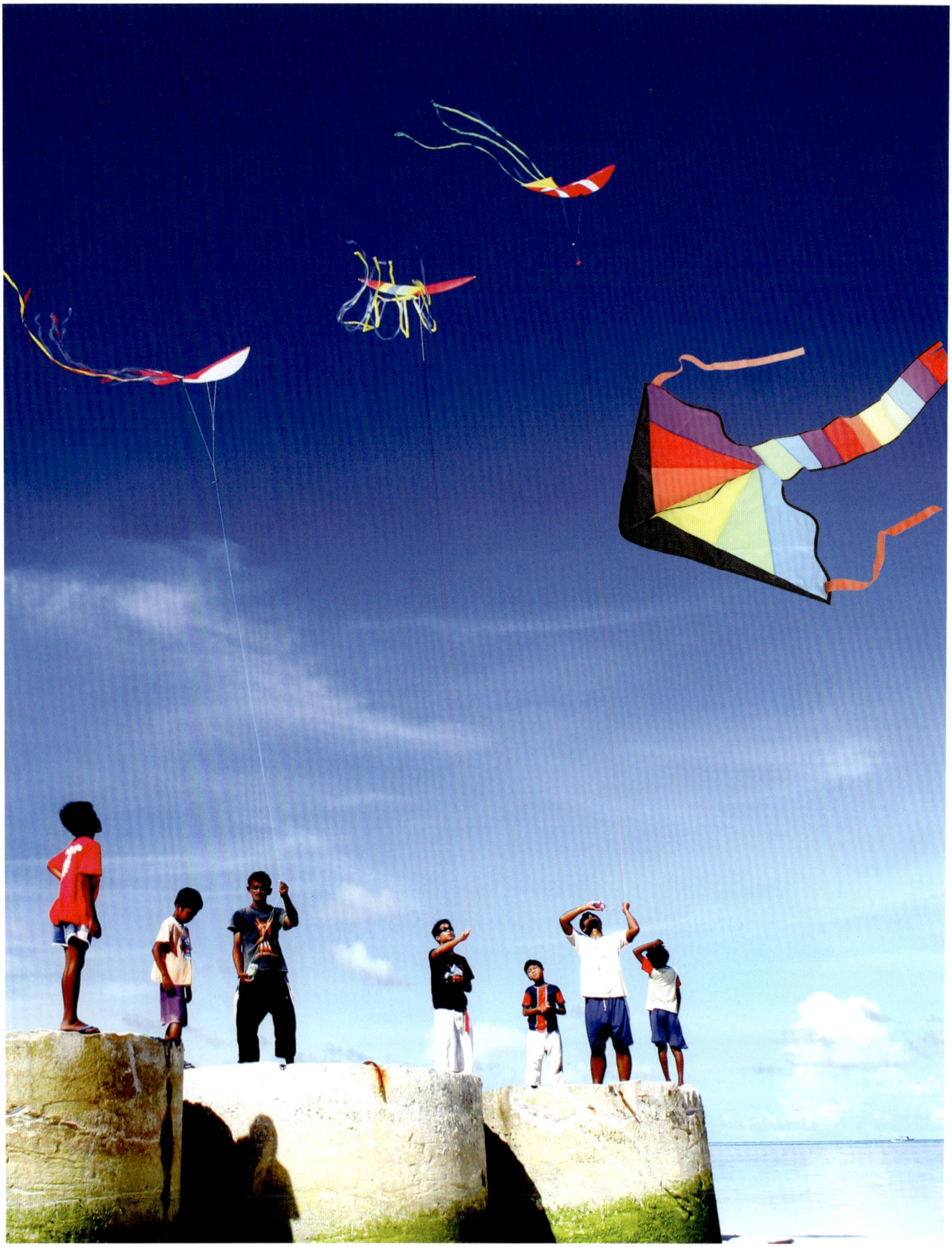